EATING THE HEART FIRST

EATING THE HEART FIRST

Poems by

Clare L. Martin

Press 53
Winston-Salem

Press 53, LLC
PO Box 30314
Winston-Salem, NC 27130

First Edition

Copyright © 2012 by Clare L. Martin

A Tom Lombardo Poetry Selection

All rights reserved, including the right of reproduction in whole or in part in any form. For permission, contact publisher at editor@Press53.com, or at the address above.

Cover design by Kevin Morgan Watson

Cover art, "He Cometh Out of the Swamp," by Pamela Womax
Copyright © 2012 by Pamela Womax,
used by permission of the artist.

Author photo by Jo Depew

Printed on acid-free paper

ISBN 978-1-935708-66-7

This book is dedicated to my husband, Dean, and our daughter Madelynne, and to my mother Lynn. It was written in memory of my father, Robert, and my son, Adam.

Out of sorrow beautiful things may come.

Acknowledgments

Poems in this collection, or early versions of them, first appeared in the following publications. Sincere thanks goes to the editors and publishers for the opportunity to present these works to the world.

Avatar Review: "Birthing" and "The Never That Was." *Blood Lotus*: "Life Expectancy." *Blue Fifth Review*: "Bread Making," "Garbage Woman" and "Mute." *Clean Sheets*: "Love in a Predawn Thunderstorm." *Dead Mule School of Southern Literature*: "Bone Woman," "Cutting," "Ice to Water," "Remembering," "Second Cup Of Coffee During a Rainstorm," "Starving Horses," "The Gift" and "To His Disquiet We Owe Recompense." *Eclectica Magazine*: "Catharsis," "Eating the Heart First" and "The Frozen Child." *Farmhouse Magazine*: "4-Way Stop at Dusk." *Glass: A Journal of Poetry*: "Winter." *Inch*: "Insomnia II." *Lily Literary Review*: "She Walks Into the Sea." *Literary Mama*: "Premature." *Melusine: Woman in the 21st Century*: "Winter Brought Out All the Knives." *Poets and Artists*: "Father Almost Drowning." *Press 1*: "Memento Mori" and "Tattoo." Press 53's *Spotlight*: "Poem Composed After Reading Plath's *Ariel* at a Junkyard," "I Have Learned To Hold My Tongue" and "Punishment." *Redheaded Stepchild*: "Lost" and "The Bird in My Ribcage." *Referential Magazine*: "Any Winter Sunday in Louisiana," "Haunted," and "The Oak Remembered from My Childhood." *Scythe*: "The Woman You Married" and "White Bull, Black Road." *Southern Hum*: "Girl Running With Horses" and "Scattering Ashes Into the Gulf of Mexico." *The Centrifugal Eye*: "Note to Self" a.k.a. ("Blue Secret.") *Thrush Poetry Journal*: "What Winter Told Me." *Wheelhouse Magazine*: "Last Night I Dreamt the Moon Was Burning." *Wild Goose Poetry Review*: "Open Me With a Fire of Words."

Recognitions

"Winter Brought Out All the Knives" was nominated for Dzanc Books' Best of the Web (2011) by *Melusine: Woman in the 21st Century*.

"Ice to Water" was nominated for *Best New Poets* 2009 and Sundress Publications *Best of the Net*, 2008, by *The Dead Mule School of Southern Literature*.

"The Bird in My Ribcage" was a 2012 selection for "Vision/Verse #4," an ekphrastic arts project by the Arts & Humanities Council of Southwest Louisiana.

"4-Way Stop at Dusk" was a finalist for the 2006 Editor's Choice Award by *Farmhouse Magazine*.

"Eating the Heart First," "Poem Composed After Reading Plath's *Ariel* at a Junkyard," "4-Way Stop at Dusk," "Tattoo," "Life Expectancy," "I Have Learned To Hold My Tongue," "To His Disquiet We Owe Recompense," "Punishment," "Starving Horses" and "The Gift" appeared in Press 53's 2011 *Spotlight* anthology.

Contents

Introduction   xi

Fables of Skin

Naked	3
Love in a Predawn Thunderstorm	4
Last Night I Dreamt the Moon Was Burning	5
Second Cup of Coffee During a Rainstorm	6
Any Winter Sunday in Louisiana	7
Poem Composed After Reading Plath's *Ariel* at a Junkyard	8
Tattoo	9
I Have Learned To Hold My Tongue	10
Bread Making	11
Bone Woman	12
The Woman You Married	13
Blue Secret	14
She Walks Into the Sea	15
What the Water Gave Me	16
Birthing	17
Girl Running With Horses	19
The Oak Remembered From My Childhood	20
Winter Brought Out All the Knives	21
The Frozen Child	22
Chasing the White Horse	23
Garbage Woman	25

A Fire of Words

Lost	29
Open Me With a Fire of Words	30
Catharsis	31
Premature	32
Eating the Heart First	33

To a Daughter Born in Winter	34
Of a Fevered Child	35
Room of Memory	36
Abandoned	37
Ice to Water	38
Starving Horses	39
The Gift	40
What Winter Told Me	41
This Is the Grave	42
The Bird in My Ribcage	43
Do Not Let Death Catch You	44
Scattering Ashes Into the Gulf of Mexico	45

All That We Conjure

White Bull, Black Road	49
Winter	50
Punishment	51
Her Body Desires the Instrument	52
Cutting	53
4-Way Stop at Dusk	54
Remembering	55
Mute	56
You, Love—	57
The Never That Was	58
These Private Hours	60
Insomnia II	61
Beloved	62
What I Long for in Dreams	63
To His Disquiet We Owe Recompense	64
Prayer of the Dreamer	65
Memento Mori	66
Muse	67
Father Almost Drowning	68
Haunted	69
Life Expectancy	70

INTRODUCTION

by Tom Lombardo, Poetry Series Editor

Imagine one of those Louisiana swamps, with the gnarly cypress trees overhanging the humid darkness, the alligators and mosquitoes both large enough to eat you alive. There is fever and fear here, but the sun's rays occasionally pierce the canopy and illuminate a wondrous cosmos that peels back to its beauty and its place on this planet.

That is the mysterious and lovely poetry of Clare L. Martin, of Youngsville, Louisiana, in her first collection.

Her searing poems search internally for an answer to the key question she poses in "These Private Hours."

>Who are we to believe this existence?

The poet tells us in her first poem "Naked" that she is *the haunted woman/ wincing at self-recognition.*

You will recognize much of her effort at self-recognition and become quite uncomfortable because Ms. Martin, when pointing her finger at herself

>On these pages I write
>only the bluest of secrets.

Ms. Martin hooks a sensual thread throughout this collection. In "Any Winter Sunday in Louisiana" the poet introduces us to

>a woman who brews
>   a hurricane
>   in her bed
>who makes love
>   as the gumbo simmers.

We can smell that gumbo. We can feel our sticky feet when this same woman *dances / in the mud of the bayou.* And we can smell the sweet cane as it *burns / against the rising moon.*

Southern poet David Bottoms in his book of essays *The Onion's Dark Core* (Press 53, 2010) notes that his mentor, the poet Dave Smith, believed there are only two subjects for poetry: life and death. Mr. Bottoms concludes that Smith is at least half right. "Actually, I think there is only one [subject]," Mr. Bottoms writes, "And every theme in literature, remote as the connection might seem, is a variation of it. The world, of course, is simply an infinite variation on death, and therefore so is the word."

Ms. Martin describes it this way in "These Private Hours":

> We gather a world.
> We become too alive in it
>
> until what is
> unknowable
>
> pierces us—

There lies the dark core of Ms. Martin's collection, this collection of poems deeply examining what she's seen of life—through her own life—on the bayous of Louisiana.

Fables of Skin

Naked

I am the woman
naked before the mirror.
I am the haunted woman
wincing at self-recognition.

I know this muscle that beats
hard in my chest
is calloused,
and grows stranger
as I know it.

I slave in the garden,
lopping mad roses,
shredding their iron tongues—
At midnight I soak
my bridal veil with gasoline
and set it afire. I dance around,
around and curse you ceremoniously.

I do not reach for you in sleep.
I keep my dream secret.
What remains is sexless, loveless.
I cannot give you what I do not have.

In a morning tryst,
my lover tells me fables of skin
and I crave you—

Love in a Predawn Thunderstorm

She had a premonition of this night.
In it, she injected undiluted love in his vein.

The muted TV glazes
the bedroom walls with prisms.

Lightning dissects the mirror.
Thunder rumbles in muscles.

She orbits his breast with her teeth,
breaks the glassy sleep encasing his body.

Breathing rain, she kisses his finger, knees.
A moth beats the windowpane between her thighs.

Last Night I Dreamt the Moon Was Burning

and cowered in its drizzling fire.
Then total blackness
beyond any darkness I'd ever known
swallowed the world.

We went down like an egg
in a snake's jaw,
past the unhinged locks,
into the belly twisted like wires,
       to a hell of acid and ice.

Second Cup of Coffee During a Rainstorm

This is my mother's land,
the house in which I was born.

On better days I walk
along paths that my feet
trod when I was growing
        into myself.

It is different now.
The cypress trees
bend in blowing rain.

The swirl of cream in my coffee
is a road opening as a mouth.
Lemon curls the edge
of the egg-smooth cup.

I thought of telling you my dream,
as the pre-dawn sky swallowed stars,
but yours was a stranger's face.
So I said,

    Unbutton me.

Will you stay in my bed when I ask?
Leave when I ask?

ANY WINTER SUNDAY IN LOUISIANA

There is a woman who brews
    a hurricane
        in her bed,
    who makes love
        as the gumbo simmers.

She is divine and divines that she is
    the circling cormorant
    that dives into marshlands
    and rivers then soars,
        leaving snaking roads
            in her wake.

Sweet cane burns
against the rising moon. She roams
    with coydogs   at midnight,
        and is witness
    to the last of the Red Wolves.

The woman dances
    in the mud of the bayou
        with alligators, nutrias
            and snakes.

In the surf of the gulf
    she scuttles: a blue crab pinching
        toes of bathers
    and rides salt-breezes—

        a gull's
        laugh on her back.

Poem Composed After Reading Plath's *Ariel* at a Junkyard

He went looking for wires
for a simulacrum
of the horse chained
to the Chevy at the junkyard—
the junkyard horse
that is starving
with only rust to eat.

But the dead are falling
out of the sky,
splattering on the road
or getting caught in leafless
branches of trees—

And he swings at those skeletons
dropping upon him
like mad—raving breathlessly
at this mad scene.

Oh, his old shins ache
from running, running, running,
but he can't shake free
from his very own bones.

And the mirror this morning
was a brittle sea
when the razor caught
his cheek in its teeth,
and there was blood
shed in the white
porcelain sink.

Tattoo

She has a tattoo
on her hip of a painted
Chinese horse—the brushstroke
animal grazes at her waist.

Black ink struggles
as if locked in wind.
In muscular unison the horse
strides to her belly:
        a field of moons.

I Have Learned To Hold My Tongue

I have learned to hold my tongue,
hold the word in my body,
that solemn space.

I've learned to be
inhabited by words.
Foster each one
as the growing child it is,
claiming it precious.

I knew the moment
I conceived,
the instance of wings
touching me.

The word *creation*
rose in my skin,
rode my nerves
like coursing love—
I spoke:
> *Not yet, not yet.*

Bread Making

The kitchen smokes
with heads of fire.
My body is a rolling
wheel, a metallic song.

Sweat pools in my arm
pits, streams under
and between my breasts.
Shoulders churn. I knead
the lump again, again.
Wring my hands red.

I am ghost-faced,
pouring out tears.
A faceless attacker, cold
hate, cores my spine
draws up my neck bone.

The feeling, black
as burnt butter,
saturates my brain.

This bread will be bitter.
It will sour and harden
those who eat it.

They will shudder
to call me mother.

Bone Woman

These bones, thin
as quills, lattices
of bone crumble so easily.

Bone-song whistles
in channels of marrow.
A pendulum swings—

O metal bearer,
mother,
sad manipulator,

        I have come here
            to pray.

Around us are holy trees,
an ancestral graveyard
        two hundred years old.

There is a silence we rail against.
There is a silence we reject—

Let me be
in those silences
that humans keep forever.

The Woman You Married

The woman you married
only salts

your meal a little
and never thins the soup.

The woman you married
mocks you with her children.

Her sons are fat and look
like their fathers. She is hollow

and rattles when she walks.
Her hands are broken

birds wresting at her hips.
The woman you married

addresses your reflection
in the mirror. She offers

only the ghost of her body—
nothing more.

Blue Secret

I have been thinking of the sea
and all it contains. Like a dream
we cannot know completely—

I am lonely. The rain
has stopped but will start again.
I taste metal in the atmosphere.

On these pages I write
only the bluest of secrets.
I remark when thunder

collapses on itself,
and when the river
embarks from the rock.

I have darkened this room.
I want sleep. Somewhere,
someone remembers my sins.

She Walks Into the Sea

She walks into the sea, out of the sea, into the sea, swinging her arms. Casting the net, her hanging breasts are like soundless bells. She crouches on an outcropping of rocks holding the line. If the nets are empty, her children will feed on night—fill their mouths with clouds, devour stars. She shovels star lit pebbles with a bare foot. She faces the moon, pulling hard. She pulls to her chest, pulls with her back, her thighs, and the muscles of her neck. Her face stiffens with anger. She breathes and desperation breaks. The haul is large, glittering. Spiked fins slap her calves. She bleeds—

Children gather for the slaughter.

What the Water Gave Me

after the painting "What the Water Gave Me" by Frida Kahlo

Before I went
      into the water
            I was not pregnant.

I would have known it.
      How can such a thing
            be unknown?

      Life exclaims itself.

But now, stretched-out
      in the bath,
      I am changed.

I know the intention
      of my womb—who or what
            creates the hushed wingbeat

I hear in my inmost mind?

Steam tongues lick my feet.
      The water is facets
            of wandering suns.

My boy, our potentialities
      are seeded in this moment.
            The vortices of our beings—
            Oh, the breadth of it!

      Bear no secret at your death,

            placid ghost, pearl-child
                  whom I shelter.

Birthing

I read your scar with my fingers
and take crushed ice
into my mouth

from a plastic cup
which has in it
the aroma of coffee.

My breasts are at their fullest
it seems, and more tender,
painful when my gown grazes

my nipples or when you've
pinched them softly. You say
how I seem a woman: full,

rounded. That we could
sprawl across this day
in the white sun of the room.

It could be hours before—
but the nurse rushes in
when the fetal heart monitor

screams. And the doctor
pierces a hole in the universe.
Water flushes out, and skin and bones.

Someone in blue
sews the stitches but I don't
feel anything except cool iodine

splashing on my inner thigh.
The old nurse cannot
unravel our weeping.

They wheel me out.
Our home is a frazzle
of livewires, explosive mines

disguised as Teddy bears,
blue blankets
and soft, tiny socks.

GIRL RUNNING WITH HORSES

The girl at the blackberry fence
feeds horses long grass of the pasture.
A wife sweats, makes bread
in a kitchen *a ways off*—

The tractor stops.
His sudden plunge spills her fear.
The girl fights oily hands.
Her mouth—stuffed too full to scream.

A running girl frightens the herd.
Beautiful horses kick in wild circles.
A girl running with horses
framed in a kitchen window startles.

The discovery is quickly
buried, never spoken.

The Oak Remembered From My Childhood

It was hollow and dying
having been struck
by lightning—

Our cousins
dared us to enter
its black maw.
Told us (and we believed)
it led
to other worlds.

Once it threatened
to fall, my uncle
doused it with gasoline
and set it on fire.

How glorious it was
to see it flame
like a living thing
against new night.

Winter Brought Out All the Knives

My offspring are gaunt
and should not be believed.

They are slaves to want.
They wake me with their mewling.

> *Give me bread.*
> *Give me a name—*

I have only this hour
and grief as a sister.

Why can't I disappear?
Or cut myself into pieces?

The Frozen Child

A boy wanders.

He stares into sunset. Forgets
the old
split tree by the creek.

He was warned
over and over.

One sad day lined up,
then another.

And snows fell.

He became still. Nothing
mothered him.
His nightmares iced.

We thought
it was *sleep* on his
bright face.

Chasing the White Horse

J. wakes
        with a head full of lights—
        flashing reds, the amber
                of caution,
starlight and fluorescence
        that burn
like the psychiatrist's stare.

J. spills over rails
        of the bunk bed
        he's slept in
        for ten years:
        too small for the legs
        of a man he's grown.

Awake, aware too of winds
        in his skull and moons
        hanging on each shoulder,
  J. stoops
  into the sink,
  splashes his face,
        rubbing soft blond stubble.

Light shocks—it's the liquid
trickling through his fingers.
Nothing   extinguishes it.

The towel smolders.

White horse whinnies at the window.
She is cloud-wash over charcoal trees.

Her mane
> teems with suns.
>> She is everything real.
>> *The world is unreal.*

That is her secret.

Chasing the white horse,
> J. is torn by branches,
>> bitten by asphalt
and singed
> with sparks cast
>> from fiery hooves.

The white horse
plunges into the river,
> boiling it pure.

Inexplicable to all,
J. dives too—

> never surfaces.

Garbage Woman

I am a gallows tree.

Bottle glass
chicken bones
jointed mannequins
of milk jug plastic

drowned oaks
crab shells
wind-struck birds
seaweed, guts and eels
        hang.

I am a body of water.

The love letters you folded
into paper boats,
sail across my hips,
burn to ash
in faraway volcanoes.

My palms weep
with pearls.

A Fire of Words

Lost

I am forgetful as a stone.

These scars
        of unknown origin—
        I cannot recall

what I have given
what has been
        given to me,

or why I am   vexed with this life
as I make a path

              to dying.

Open Me With a Fire of Words

I long for the quiet hour: the hour
within the hour, the hour within
myself in which my self
expands with quiet,
into quiet.

I am stilled, then, to hear
the resonance
of a stirring word— the words

thrumming *yes*
against the solar plexus,
this knife of the sun,
this the pronouncement of lightning

engendered in me
in the quiet hour,
in the exquisite,
quiet hour.

Catharsis

The planet is strapped to my back. Moons jiggle in my stomach. I'm making fists, clenching my toes, tightening my urethra—beating walls fist-marked. Pulling electrical wires does no good. Give me an orgasm. My cries will crack the iron locking my gut shut. I need a long drive on a black road, a wildfire. Birds fly in smoke. The scattering deer look beautiful and scared.

Premature

The fetal body breaks loose
becomes a little boat
tethered to a harbor of machines.

Doctors say the hearts
of these children whisper-tick
like doll hearts: inconsistently.

Death can come as a whisper
blown across the cheek.

He will always be frail.

He has his father's
un-feathered skin
and the bones of birds
that were my visitors
during a trimester of sleep.

Born to fit in my purse,
he is one singing coin
among many.

Eating the Heart First

Her body bristles.

She hears the plucked string,
the whoosh of arrow—

When she is felled,
you must eat the heart first.

It is a hellish flower.
Cut it out whole. Its pulse fills your hand.

She will talk in your skin.
Her fear will mingle with your own.

Cold, you sleep.
Your dreams flood with moons.

Wolves hunt this night of your mind,
keep you running.

To a Daughter Born in Winter

This night in my arms
you look into my eyes

with something I imagine is love
but Daughter, I know it is

hunger,
hunger.

I will keep this place for you,
cover your wounds

and heal you. The lullaby
I sing is garbled in sobs.

Everything becomes dust—
even you, even me.

You were born in winter
and winter holds you.

Outside the wind is fretting.
Silver leaves fall

like tattered letters that drift
out of a mother's hands.

Of a Fevered Child

What is in her body
      cannot pass through
cannot   escape
skin or the   blood

winding through her
          the virus
is tying up   her little fingers
white-wide stare at

the ceiling   she moans
hot breathing,
      her cheek
      hot-as-a-biscuit

her eyes
      grayer
the sun forgets her
      silk-thin veins

red light her eyes
          the cement chill—
      and still I hold her
to account.

Room of Memory

for Kim, after Chiharu Shiota's "Room of Memory"

O glass palace,
wood-boned mother—

let us enter, our hands
ungloved, and touch

your ethereal center.
Inside you, we weep

at the recollection of pain.
How the knife

broke on bone.
And we choked

as though the air
itself was a cold spike.

We are captives, now,
of a fallible tongue.

Bled of all strength,
we are awed

by your silence:
        a sleeping crow,
        a stillborn.

Abandoned

I begged you to come

to the black hill,
to the screaming river

to wash our baby down,
to cure her of a fever.

I wanted you with me:

> your face a bright ember,
> your tongue ready to conspire—

But you did not come

so I burned down
our house stick-by-stick

and whirled around the fire
singing a blasphemy.

And I will follow
the lashings of smoke

to the high places
and the low

until I find from what
beast this airy blood beats.

What are these words
but weapons of grief?

My bridesmaids are dead,
forever-keeping secrets.

I have none left
to wrest from my tongue.

ICE TO WATER

The hospital room is cool.
There are moths in your breath.

Circled in ice, you're enwrapped in white fire.
Coffee-colored urine drains in a bag.

I swab your lips with lemon glycerin.
Your pulse beeps loss. I buzz a nurse out of the void.

I cannot watch you die.
The doctor scowls at my cowardliness.

Stunted from birth, plucked too early—
You were wingless.

It took me years to believe it wasn't my fault
you despaired in an infant's life.

I choose blue for the burial
like the thunderhead in your eyes.

The undertaker powders the fine
hairs of your face, seals you in secret.

Starving Horses

I see it in the cliffs of bone
at her shoulder and flank,
and in her opaque eyes.

It is late winter and blood-warm
breath clouds in the light
as I load grandfather's Winchester.

For a week she'll rot
until the backhoe arrives
under a calligraphic line of trees.

My muscles ache to pull
earth over hoof and hair.

I can't decide what to uncover,
or hide of neglect
and early frost.

The Gift

Here is a vein.
I *want* you to have it.
It was harvested near bone.
Oxygen transmutes it.
Press it hard. Do you hear thunder?
It is filled with it.

I am giving it to you. Take it.
I care not what you do—

Leave it
by the roadside to mark
an automobile wreck, a highway exchange.
Give it as change. Press it
between pages as you would a leaf
or a flower given by a lover.

Rewrite its history.

What Winter Told Me

If I raise my voice above a whisper the world will shatter. Be patient—dark is coming. It is only for a time that you are mine. You have forgotten the names of your children, their radiant paths. In me, you will know barrenness. With bleak power I cleanse an impure world. Bare yourself upon the bed and wait for the one you love. He is climbing a tree. He is taking the belt from his robe to hang himself dead. With my winds, I will cut him down, close his eyes. Shake the storm out of him, for you.

This Is the Grave

The earth will hold you as I cannot.
Let your bones go to her. The earth,

your other mother, will coddle you—
her charges will enter you softly.

They worm through your sinews,
devouring vessels.

I would not leave you
to the callous birds. I would not

expose you to that harrowing night.
I would not send you to a water-doom.

The river's teeth will not mar you.
Now go deeply into the loam.

Go to the place I have secured for you,
          for your rest.

The Bird in My Ribcage

The bird
        in my ribcage
                flutters
like a heart.

It dances,
        pecking the fig
                in my throat.

The wild-weeds
        and vines
                tangled
to my spine
        are its nesting place.

It drinks
        from the well
                of my womb.

Do Not Let Death Catch You

or the ocean take you
into spiraled caverns

where no living
thing sees light.

Fill your lungs.
Rise from this,

the darkest water.
Let the wind

carry you
on ethereal bones.

Be of the grass,
of dreaming birds.

Be of the last unforgiving
stone of the silent earth.

Fire scatters your wish.
Burning petals of ash

drift to your cheek—
Remember

when your mind was keen,
when the hope

which possessed you
rose to the stars.

Scattering Ashes Into the Gulf of Mexico

Storm-light cracks the rain-whipped windshield.
We are numbed by the beat of the blades and grief.

Your childhood was a shattered peace. Memories cut on broken hearts.
When your father left, life derailed into a crushing wreck.

Strangers you called "uncle" streamed after the bars closed.
You soothed yourself with lies. You showed her mercy, love.

Your mother wanted to be drunk when she died. She reeked of urine.
You gave her vodka on ice. It kissed her like morphine.

Your inheritance is a collection of rings, none made of gold.
She bequeathed mysteries for your mourning.

In slashing rain, you seek a point on the storm-dark horizon to take you
into a sweet memory of her, but she is obscure, inscrutable.

You offer ashes to the thunder and wind.
That death is our singular future gives you peace.

Assured the moon will still pull these gulf waves
even when no one loved is left living.

# All That We Conjure

White Bull, Black Road

White bulls
rise like sacrificial smoke,
crossing the black

road in dead-dark night.
Ride on, ride on savior
in blood-thick rain, I pray,

you will go to your sleep
in peace. This fitful night
of white winds and white

bulls crossing black roads,
I do not inhabit my body.
I left it behind to drift

like ash over rivers,
across wildwoods and fields,
littering highways with stars.

Winter

I will tell you

of ice and dusk,
of the long night
we burned our love letters

in a warming fire
and my grandmother's
bed became kindling.

See my thin dress,

my brittleness?
I have begged leaves
not to fall.

Trees harsh as skeletons—

eviscerated to black
sway in white winds:
        a fever-dance.

Punishment

We find the child's skeleton,
browned, bare of skin or muscle,

when we sweep dead brush away.
There is a bird skeleton

too, along the path, small,
sharp-beaked.

Driving the mountain,
clouds feather the radiant sun.

We turn the car
to the plowed drive.

The woman tells us
she had filled his lungs

with her own breath, twice,
three times—She had been

milking the cow,
picking the fresh eggs

and noticed the bare tree,
the black, spindly branch:
        the perfect switch.

Her Body Desires the Instrument

She elongates herself.
Presses the instrument

against her body,
as in the dream

that comes to her
and comes to her—

The old guitar crumbles.
Strings fall in tonal

disarray. The wooden
neck becomes chalk

crushed in her grip.
She longs to be soothed

by melodies which flutter
from her mind

to her lips,
to her fingertips.

She feels percussion
in her spine.

Drumming in muscles,
a rhythm resounds

that could vanquish
the dark spell.

Her body desires
the instrument

and she despairs
without accompaniment.

Cutting

I've taken cuttings of roses
and grown them
into ravishing bushes.

It seemed a simple thing
but took constant attention—
adoption of the flower
into myself.

It bit my hands. Bloomed wildly
fed on my blood.

Life is like this—
constantly feeding.

I've been forced
to disinherit my children,
send them into winter.

If I had not,
they would have
bled me dry.

4-Way Stop at Dusk

Little birds, little pirates plotting
murder on the wire
crave *bloodwine*—their flight
impresses a watermark
on my soul, dusts
sunset with silhouettes.

Twilight is a pearl
crushed in a raptor's claw.
The kestrel's razor wing
bleeds the field.

Remembering

Bicycling River Road,
we topped the levee
shoveled there to brace
the bayou and coasted down.

We spun past horses
kicking wildly as if they too
sensed the shift of earth and sky.

We rode the length
of fence to watch them.
The soft sun enflamed the river.

I wanted to wander that land
on horseback a hundred years prior
when the soil was undisturbed,
when the live oaks
stood their ground undiminished.

To ride through gold
grasses of the Louisiana prairie,
flushing meadowlarks and bobwhites
from their ground roosts.

I, on the sorrel mare
and you on the appaloosa,
stunning and speckled-dark
like the becoming sky,
would ride for one hundred years
      and never forget.

MUTE

Hands like flushed doves
flutter to say: *dry the dishes*—

sweep the floor, but never *be quiet*.
When she went blind, too,

we spelled *goodnight* and *I love you* tenderly,
tracing each alphabet

on the scattered leaves of her palms.
I married and she touched

my hips, spreading her hands wide
to note I was getting fat. She patted

my growing belly
but never cradled my offspring.

When the infant died,
pantomime cries

fell like trees
in storms from her mouth.

You, Love—

Illuminate my dark
with your tongue's improvisation.

Resonate in my body,
in my arms, my neck and thighs.

Do not warn me of your movements.

Enlighten my skin,
cup me and clench me.

I give up my salt to you.

I am your range, your territory.
My vulnerability is yours solely.

I fear no danger with you.

Give me the determination of your mouth
and my hips will pitch to you.

Our sex is a wave,
wind over wildflower fields,
a wild road—

I am your disciple.

The Never That Was

I have not one picture
of us taken in Barcelona,

or Carcassonne. None
from the Mediterranean

summer when you rubbed
my bare skin with creams,

carefully around the areolas
so they would not burn,

or of you in the morning
laughing and gesturing

with the old French couple
standing in the sea casting nets.

And at dusk you fed me summer
fruit with your woodsman fingers,

and we drank wine as though
we'd stolen into a still life.

I close my eyes and see you
leaning pose-like,

pressing a calloused palm
on the stone of the cathedral.

In sun-filled rooms,
beneath cool sheets,

we aligned our naked bodies.
'Blackbird fly blackbird fly'

you sang until I fell asleep–
We met for the first time

the following spring.
This is verifiable.

That you were always with me
is truth, as well.

These Private Hours

All that we conjure:

the animal cravings—
our unrequited lusts

will be relinquished.

Who are we to believe this existence?

We gather a world.
We become too alive in it

until what is
unknowable

pierces us—

Insomnia II

These sleepless nights are blades.
I'm awake as birth.

All these hours I set fire
to plastic kings,
bulldoze their castles—I'm due

a fuck-hard retribution,
a comeuppance—

and I am waiting for it
to kick in
any minute now.

Beloved

Give me a thousand names
      and call to each.

All I am is yours,
      yet in you I become

undone by this force
      which exists
         beyond feeling,

encompasses dualities,
all potentialities—

Illuminate the dark room of my heart.
      Pierce it with suns—

I am yours.   *I am yours.*

      I am afraid

to touch the core
      of what I mean to say.

What I Long for in Dreams

I am learning the instrument, pouring myself into the instrument onto the keys, through to the tight wires, creating sound.

I innately know the instrument and can perform masterpieces of original composition. I can translate what I long for into sounds executed on the instrument.

There is a room which houses the instrument. The roof of our house is a sieve and the voices of strangers rain over us.

Exposed, the instrument's lacquered finish buckles and peels—but I play furiously with precision, in dreams, only in dreams.

My whole body is attuned. I shudder with rhythm. I am a virtuoso, abusing the keyboard with bruising passion—

I am the dreamer, always the dreamer, mourning a dismal sleep.

To His Disquiet We Owe Recompense

The priest anoints
the old father and gives
Last Rites, then sits
with the wife in her kitchen
to hear a mournful
confession.

The grown son times
the residue of heartbeat,
until there is nothing to hear
with an ear on the chest
or feel with a finger.

In a year, mother and son
will notice the silk
iris in the bronze
vase atop the gravestone,
once so purple-plush,
is now hued like a vein
under the thinnest,
wan skin.

Prayer of the Dreamer

Dark-dreaming sea, you are refuge—
        Place the silver
        of your worth   in my palm.

Emboss me   with a fever-touch,
        then I will become

soul and body

        dizzied with you,
        unbound,
        washed in sweet
                exhalations.

Soul-huntress,
            do not throw me
        into the dust.

Dust settles upon dust
            upon the dust
            of everything.

Memento Mori

A man walks across water
on stones. Notices a crow
sinking in the blue sky.

He steps onto earth,
leaning momentarily
against a cedar sapling.
Pines etch and sway.
The creek laughs. The man thinks
of endings and beginnings—
his youngest daughter's
daisy-eyes.

He slips his hand into his pocket,
fingering the dry skull
of a hummingbird. And it is cold
spring again: the iridescent
hummingbird is caught
in a spider's web.

The spider silk enwrapping
the tiny bird holds bones together.
He picks at the feathers
sodden with rot.

He opens like a fan
the thin-as-paper wings.
Bones disarrayed, drift
to the ground in silence.

Muse

We marry into grief
and the poems pile

up against our ribs.
Secrets hold to us

and we hold to them.
We are bound to endings

as the culmination
of light binds us.

Darkness: a berry,
blood on the tongue—

It has been a long time
since we have written poetry.

Why do we wait?
Fault-lines split the earth.

The ink of the crow
marks the cloud—

Shall we not muse
upon its bantering wings?

Father Almost Drowning

You—a boy
nearly drowning

went into the body
of darkness,

and darkness held to you.
Mud rose to blind you.

Silken weeds
flourished in your lungs.

Branches of sunken trees
made wounds of your ankles.

And when your uncle's hand
fished you out,

the Bayou Vermilion
bled out of your mouth.

Still, rusted cars
sleep demolished

on the banks
and all things green die.

Haunted

I am kept by crows.
They beckon out of sleep,

calling come, come
be transformed.

Crow-by-crow
line up in dreams,

punctuating visions.
Such an omen inspires.

A crow told me:

>Let me be a whorl of darkness—
>Let me be a fist in the sun.

The crow on the wire
is a keeper of silence.

What a crow gathers
becomes soot and nothing more.

I am in the night. I am in it
as though it cloaks me—

I am winged
and feathered like the crow.

Sheer, yet impenetrable,
rising on wind.

Life Expectancy

The nurse at my side has no love.
She watches TV, eats Chinese & takes my pills—
Switches my sopped diaper for a fresh
one just before the next sitter arrives.

She tells me crows are eating fat, purple figs.
Gently takes my hand, slips off my rings.
Dropped in her purse, they clink like coins.

I am a moon in the mirror. I've forgotten my face.
I have two bodies. One is a cold trap.
The other is a mist over the bed, a beaded pain.

I can't remember if I have children.
If I did, they would be stones.
I have only slivers of memories—
a dark-eyed girl
follows a ghost into a bathroom,
is knocked into a dream.

In the shower
she flows to the drain.

A Note from the Author

I would like to thank Amy Waguespack, Kelly Clayton and Patrice Melnick who guided me in the shaping of this book. I also want to thank Darrell Bourque for the wonderful wisdom and support given to me without expecting anything but friendship. I give thanks to Kevin Morgan Watson and Tom Lombardo for believing in this work and bringing it to the world. So many friends have encouraged my writing. I am indebted to them all. Of course, I give enduring thanks to my family for being the net beneath my aerial act.

CLARE L. MARTIN is a graduate of the University of Louisiana at Lafayette and lifelong Louisiana resident. Her poetry has appeared in numerous literary journals and anthologies, both online and in print, including *Avatar Review*, *Blue Fifth Review*, *Literary Mama*, *Louisiana Literature*, and *Poets and Artists*. Her poems have been included in the anthologies *The Red Room: Writings from Press 1*, *Best of Farmhouse Magazine* Vol. 1, and *Beyond Katrina*. Her work has been nominated for Dzanc Books' Best of the Web (2011), Best New Poets (2009), and Sundress Publication's Best of the Net (2008 and 2011). She was one of three poets appearing in the 2011 *Spotlight* anthology published by Press 53.

Cover artist **PAMELA WOMAX** is an amateur photographer who was born and raised in a small southern town along the bayous of south Louisiana. Pamela says her goal as a photographer is to capture the surreal beauty that south Louisiana has to offer. She now resides in a small town outside of New Orleans.

See more of Pamela's work at www.flickr.com/photos/pamelaya9/

www.ingramcontent.com/pod-product-compliance
Lightning Source LLC
Chambersburg PA
CBHW022108040426
42451CB00007B/178